WHO NEEDS THE CHURCH?

WHO NEEDS THE CHURCH?

The 1982 Barclay Lectures

GERALD PRIESTLAND

THE SAINT ANDREW PRESS
EDINBURGH

First published in 1983 by
THE SAINT ANDREW PRESS
121 George Street, Edinburgh EH2 4YN

Copyright © Gerald Priestland, 1983

ISBN 0 7152 0553 6

Printed by William Blackwood & Sons Ltd., Edinburgh

CONTENTS

Preface   vii

1 The Church in the Street   1

2 The Church in the World   25

3 The Church in the Air   43

PREFACE

Many people the world over remember William Barclay as the supreme communicator of the New Testament in their time. When he retired in 1974 from his Professor's Chair at Glasgow University, a few of his personal friends, myself among them, organised a "Tribute to William Barclay" rally in Wellington Church, Glasgow. Simultaneously we gave his large public the opportunity to contribute to a testimonial fund. Our wish was that this fund should be employed to create a fitting and enduring memorial to his remarkable work as teacher, preacher, writer and broadcaster. It was with William Barclay's own enthusiastic approval, if not in fact at his suggestion, that we decided to use the money raised to found a lectureship – The Barclay Lectureship in Communication of the Christian Gospel.

The first lecturer was David Sheppard, Bishop of Liverpool, who gave his lectures in 1978. William Barclay was a party to this choice of lecturer but, sadly, died before the lectures came to be delivered. The second lecturer – in 1980 – was Robin Barbour, Professor of New Testament Exegesis at Aberdeen University and Moderator of the General Assembly in 1979.

This book is the text of the third series of Barclay Lectures, delivered by Gerald Priestland in

November 1982. It was with much delight that my fellow-trustees and I received his acceptance of our invitation to give these lectures. Gerald Priestland is one who has demonstrated both in his writing and in his broadcasting that he, too, is a brilliant communicator. The present volume is further evidence of that already well-established fact, and I am extremely happy to have the opportunity to wish it well.

James Martin,
Chairman of the Barclay Lectureship Trustees
(High Carntyne Church, Glasgow).

1

THE CHURCH IN THE STREET

I am so appalled by the task before me, in delivering these lectures, that you must forgive my wasting as much time as possible in not doing it. So, for the next few minutes, I will pay my tributes, make my excuses, test your sympathy, prepare my escape route – do anything but tackle the subject in hand, and with good reason. For it must be abundantly clear to anyone who has been idle enough to read my books or listen to my broadcasts that I have no qualifications whatever to be addressing you. Or rather, I have only one: and that is the foolhardiness to express, sometimes, the doubts and fears that many of us share about religion. It is thought to be "not done" for a preacher (which is what I suppose I am) to display his weakness. He is supposed to give strength to the faltering and direction to those who have gone astray. But all I can hope to do is to give courage to my fellow seekers after truth by sharing with them my weakness, and showing that it is still possible to call oneself a Christian without having passed an official examination in Christianity.

Would William Barclay have agreed with that – with all his scholarship and distinction in the academic world? I am quite sure he would: not just

1

because he was a fellow broadcaster, and a churchman who never thought it beneath him to make the faith comprehensible to ordinary people, but because he remained on the side of the publicans and sinners – not of the scribes and Pharisees. He was a very human man – more so, perhaps, than I am.

It is an alarming thing to start out, as he did and I did, doing what looks like a fairly humdrum job; and then to find that something is happening – a response from the public – that transforms it into something one had never intended or wanted. In William Barclay's case, he shouldered the cross and bore it to the end: in mine, I have to plead guilty to a lack of resolution and of stamina. I have retired from the full-time job of Media Guru, and I am only here today because I promised to be a long time ago. The final straw came when Dr Edward Norman, Dean of Peterhouse, Cambridge, announced that the British people had deposed the Archbishop of Canterbury and elected me as spiritual leader of the nation. Knowing Dr Norman, I do not think that was meant as a compliment either to me or the Archbishop; but it was a cue to back out of the limelight, and I took it. In Scotland, you will not be so easily deceived anyway.

I am not a total stranger to the Scottish churches and their ways. My wife's family and my mother's were Presbyterians, and many are the hours I have spent enthralled by the proceedings of the General Assembly (unkindly known in my trade as "The Black and White Ministers' Show"). Nevertheless, I had better make it clear from the start that most of my generalisations during these lectures will be drawn from experience of the churches south of the border and elsewhere: thus enabling you to comfort yourselves, during any uncomfortable passage, with the thought that "He can't be referring to *us*"! If the cap fits, you can always claim it belongs to somebody else with the same size head.

Finally, by way of excuse, I should declare what most of you will already know, that I am personally a Quaker – a member of the non-dogmatic, non-liturgical, non-sacramental (in other words, heretical) Religious Society of Friends. I have not always been so. I was brought up a Public School Anglican, moved into the English Presbyterians because the sermons were better, and took to Quakerism when it occurred to me that quieter surroundings might give me a chance to hear what God, rather than Man, was trying to say. That is as true tonight, of course, as it ever was.

You will know that the Society of Friends was founded in the mid-seventeenth century as a reaction from the institutional Church. The early Quakers revolted against what they saw as the effort to organise and codify the movement of the Holy Spirit, to substitute an imposed faith for one directly experienced. It may seem odd – and perhaps rather suspicious – that I should have chosen for my subject in these lectures "The Church", which I have subdivided into "The Church in the Street" (by which I mean in everyday life), "The Church in the World" (by which I mean the wider life of politics and economics), and "The Church in the Air" (by which I mean the field of broadcasting and communications). Why should I

care about the Church, when I belong to a Society
with neither ministers nor moderators nor bishops?
Indeed, I have chosen as my front-page headline
the challenge "Who needs the Church?"

Do you? Do I? Does God? Does anybody need
the Church except the Church itself? Has it ever
been anything but a gigantic confidence trick, a
home for old ladies and gentlemen, a career
structure for sentimental wets, surviving on a
mixture of superstition, toadyism and spiritual
blackmail; besides wasting vast sums of money on
functionless architecture, beside which the palaces
of royalty look a minor extravagance? Not to
mention the crusades and persecutions, the wars of
religion, the inquisitions and heresy hunts, the
martyrdoms and book-burnings. Who needs a
Church like this? Was this what Jesus of Nazareth
had in mind – Jesus who walked the hills of
Palestine, teaching in the open air, sharing his
bread and wine with his friends, and passing on his
gospel not to the priestly caste of Israel but to
twelve ordinary working men? And what did he say
to them about the way they should organise
themselves?

"Be not ye called Rabbi: for one is your Master,
even Christ; and all ye are brethren.

And call no man your father upon the earth; for
one is your Father, which is in Heaven.

Neither be ye called masters, for one is your
Master, even Christ. But he that is greatest among
you shall be your servant."

Is that the Church as it came to be? Is that the
blueprint for this hierarchy that haunts us still, of
Popes and Patriarchs, Bishops and Archbishops,

Moderators, Archimandrites, Priors, Provosts and Prebendaries? Jesus said, "Where two or three are gathered together in my name, there am I in the midst of them". He did not say, ". . . provided one of them is an ordained priest within the apostolic succession" nor even ". . . provided one of them has an Edinburgh degree in Divinity and subscribes to the Westminster Confession".

So who needs this Church? Apparently *I* do not need it, since all a Quaker needs is a simple room, a gathering of friends, and an hour or so of silence. As I have said, we have no minister, no set form of worship, no sacraments daily, weekly or monthly. Mind you, most people find this so profoundly unsatisfactory that we can barely raise twenty thousand members in the United Kingdom. But as we have managed to keep going for the past three hundred years, there does seem to be *prima facie* evidence of the ability to survive without even a Gothic arch or a crucifix in sight.

Do *you* need the Church? I suppose the fact that you are here now is some evidence that the Church serves a useful purpose as an entertainment manager. But you could have heard me – or better than me – on radio or television; and if I may say so, my books are available still at bargain prices. If you want to hear a voice crying in the wilderness, you do not actually have to venture into the wilderness any more.

And does *God* need the Church? Obviously, if there *is* a God, he will be there whether there are men dressed like women going through strange motions at the altar or not. The fact that so many people doubt whether there is a God suggests to me that the Church has not been doing a particularly good job for him, anyway. Surely that must be the first duty of his Church: to proclaim, convince and show God's very existence. And if it fails in that, why should he need it? There may be better ways. What real use does God have for ancient buildings, dreary hymns and a nod from us once a week? Better, perhaps, to tear it all down and force those who want God to go out and find him in the streets and shops and factories, where he is busy seven days a week. Who needs the Church?

As a matter of fact, I do, and you do, and God (I suspect) would at least rather have it than not. As for the Church itself, in the rather derogatory terms in which I have been describing it, I guess it would be only too glad to disappear. It does not need that kind of life, and it is actually we who have forced it upon the Church. It would rather be something else. It would rather be what Christ has called it to be, but it is we who will not allow it. The sad thing is that, while most of the church leadership keeps saying to its people: "We know we have got to get out of the rut and change; only tell us what you want, help us to renew the Church", too many lay people respond by backing away from the invitation, or turn childishly to authoritarian religion. It seems that many people still need that kind of Church as a refuge from reality, a return to the spiritual nursery, with Nanny on hand to read the old fairy tales and nursery rhymes. But I am afraid it cannot survive what is going on in the rest of the house. The Holy Spirit is determined to blow the nursery sky high and force the children to grow up. I believe we saw part of this scheme in England recently, when the General Synod of the Church of England rejected the Covenant for Unity with the Methodists and the United Reformed Church. There had been much ado about the apostolic succession, women priests and joint decision-making at the top. But "Rubbish!" cried the Holy Spirit, "You've got to start at the bottom! That's where I am, among the people! Unless Anglicans and Methodists and United Reformed are actually working and worshipping together in the parishes, I don't care two hoots whether you turn a moderator into a bishop or put a cardinal into the Coronation service. It's the Church we are talking about, not a corporate management structure!"

I do not actually think the Holy Spirit spends much time in the General Synod of the Church of England – nor, for that matter, in the General Assembly of the Church of Scotland. He has never mastered the committee system, and I suspect he is more of a demagogue than a democrat. I think he is busy elsewhere, instigating all kinds of subversive activities, from way-out theology at St Andrews and Cambridge, to the Movement for the Ordination of Women, to illicit intercommunions and do-it-yourself baptisms. Appalling! Sometimes even risky. But a warning to the conventional churches that talking down to the people from above is far less important than being down there among them, listening. The Church has got to listen, if it wants to know where it is being called.

For the Church, of course, is really the people – the children and followers of God. Manses and moderators, sermons and synods are the mere packaging of this people, perhaps inevitable, anyway historical, but not to be mistaken for the thing itself. The thing itself, the believing and worshipping people, has two important character-istics which the individual Christian must never forget. The Church is a community, and it is a continuity. And here I get down to defending what I have been savaging up to now.

For in spite of my exasperation with the Church – and my membership of a Society which many regard as outside it – I do revere the Church and thank God for it. And I insist upon regarding the Society of Friends as a lay order within the One Great Church – a contemplative side-chapel with-in the great cathedral, contributing now and then a few bars of silence to the worship which is constantly in progress. Quakers may be an ex-perimental sect – both in the modern sense of pushing forward the frontiers of faith, and in the older sense of insisting upon experience as the basis of their faith – but if we are honest we must admit that we build upon the foundations laid for us over many centuries by the Church.

I have lately been arguing to my fellow Quakers (to the horror of some of them) that we ought not to shun the traditional doctrines of the Church as if they were chains to shackle our spirits. We should regard them as climbing-ropes to help us up the mountain, as tools with which to handle and carve out our experience. Doctrines, I think, are not unreasonable certainties. They are reasonable uncertainties, and without them it is very hard to explore the kingdom of faith or even to discuss it at all. It is *possible* to make music without adopting the established conventions of time and key and harmony; but they are based upon real characteristics, and if you abandon them you put yourself at the disadvantage of cutting yourself off from the support of the past. So it is with the doctrines of the Church.

So I think we need the Church for its continuity, for the insights and conventions it has handed down. After all, we have no right to assume that the saints and fathers of the Church were all idiots, and that we are the first generation to have seen things as they really are. Certainly we are facing a world very different from that of the saints and fathers. We have to ask ourselves constantly: What must the truth be *now* if people who thought as they did wrote as they did? We must have the courage to interpret. But if poets like Sophocles and Horace can still speak truth to us, why not saints like Augustine and Julian? The human condition has changed, but not out of all recognition.

Above all, we need the Church for the *stories* it hands down to us, and these are terribly important to Christians, because of our Jewish origin. The Jews are compulsive story-tellers: compare the Bible with the Koran, and instead of the continuous harangues and exhortations of the latter, the Bible emerges as one long story. The great thing about a story is that it is not dogmatic: it concerns the reaction of human beings to their circumstances. It is open-ended: it implies things going on even after the story has finished, and its significance for the reader develops with every passing day. There have been times when I saw the importance of the Prodigal Son story in terms of the willingness of the father to forgive; at others I have

seen it as the freedom he gave the Prodigal to go
out and make his mistakes; at others as the need of
the sinner to turn towards home in order to secure
forgiveness; at others again, as the need of the
righteous brother to accept the father's apparent
unfairness. These are all there in the story, and I
have no doubt I shall find other significances as
time goes by. But only a story could have wrapped
them all up together and kept each one waiting for
the time I needed it.

The Church has done us an enormous service in
preserving and publishing our stories about God,
and doing its conscientious best to see that they
have come down to us in a remarkably uncontamin-
ated form. Which is not to say there has not been
some fiddling with the text. But the more we learn
through scholarship, the more remarkable it is how
little there has been. I am afraid the admirers of
Gnostic gospels get little sympathy from me: not
simply because their mysteries belong to another
world from that of the Canon, but because I cannot
make sense of a Jesus who came for the humble and
meek and then, if we are to believe the Gnostics,
concealed his message in code language. Whatever
it is, the Christian Church is not a secret society,
and we owe it a great debt of gratitude for keeping
its doors wide open, its message accessible to all. It
could so easily have been otherwise, and there are
still some who would have it so.

I have been accused, with some justice, of
over-emphasising the rational appeal of Christianity; of presenting it too much as a matter of the
head and not enough of the heart. I suppose this is a
question of personal temperament. In fact my

instinctive awareness of God's presence – my trust
in his love – is so much a wall-to-wall feature of my
life that I hardly find it necessary to mention. In this
scientific – or, too often, pseudo-scientific – age, I
am more anxious, perhaps, to meet head-on what
many people regard as reasoned objections to
faith. If I wanted to speak from the heart, I suppose
I would have to write music or poetry for you, and
that would be hard to argue with. One overwhelm-
ing reason why I personally need the Church is that
I need its religious language to express and explore
the apprehension that I have of God: experiences
that are undeniably there, which I find to be shared
by others, and which can only be handled (however
imperfectly) by the language the Church has
evolved.

But I am well aware that the Church has always
spoken another language beside that of theology,
and that to many Christians this is even more
important than the language of words – I mean the
language of the sacraments.

Perhaps I am treading on thin ice, here among
the people of Knox and Calvin. Is Priestland tilting
towards Rome? Not tilting, I think, but visiting –
as, on my pilgrim way I claim the right to visit
Canterbury and Geneva, Swarthmore and Nor-
wich, Constantinople and Jerusalem, too, if I
please. And, as I do so, I find as many good
Christians who draw grace from the signs and
gestures of the Church as I do those who draw it
from the words of scripture. More significant still, I
find churches which were once aggressively scriptu-
ral placing more emphasis on the sacraments, and
churches which were once almost exclusively

sacramental paying more and more attention to scripture. For example, you may have noticed that during Pope John-Paul's visit to Great Britain his addresses were as rich in biblical texts as a cake is with currants: there was hardly one of them that could not have been delivered by Billy Graham. On the other hand, in many Anglican churches today – even of the Lowest tendency – Holy Communion is far more frequent than it was forty years ago. Now, whatever your feelings may be about that in Scotland, there is no doubt in my mind that sacramentalism can and does feed many souls at a depth which nothing else reaches: and for this again, the Church must be thanked.

Once again, you may think it curious for a Quaker to be saying this; for, as I have said, we use no sacraments. That is not to say no Quaker ever takes the sacraments elsewhere. I do so myself when I feel it is right, and when I am sure my action will not be misunderstood by others or give offence to them. I have been deeply moved and strengthened by sharing the Lord's Supper in the High Kirk in Edinburgh. It seemed to me an affirmation that we *are* all one, in spite of our quibbles. And like those *stories* about God, the sacraments (those *actions* about God) are in themselves non-dogmatic: they simply *are*, and no minister on earth can prevent their meaning to you or me what they mean to you or me. They, too, are free and open-ended. To insist that they can only have one meaning is like insisting that when a bird flies up from a tree it must necessarily fly south. Birds fly in all directions, or the Highlands and Islands would be birdless; and if we are to have a God who is more

than two-dimensional, his love must be
apprehended from many points of view. Which is
why, within the Church, there are churches.

You may gather from this that I have my
reservations about the so-called "Scandal of Disun-
ity". May there not also be a Scandal of
Uniformity – a diminishing, a standardising of
God and his worship? Certainly there has been –
and still is – a Scandal of Uncharitableness among
Christians, a readiness to denounce other Christian
groups as little better than pagans; and I would
sooner see that stamped out before we engage in
further schemes for organisational unity. And –
praise the Lord – it *is* being stamped out among
the older churches. The coming-together is patchy,
varying from community to community, limited in
some places to social activities, spreading in others
to study groups and Sunday schools. I know it is
already a lively issue here in Scotland, and a thorny
one at that, but it seems to me the formation of
joint Christian schools is becoming a matter of
some urgency, before the moral element in our
children's education is completely washed away by
the secular flood. If the churches, acting as One
Church, will not undertake this – who else possibly can?

I think I must resist the temptation here to wade
into the general issue of Ecumenism and the
dialogue about doctrine. One reason why I am not
really scandalised by the variety of churches is that
it does offer the Christian pilgrim a series of
stepping stones along which he can move; for I
really see no shame in passing through several
churches during a lifetime – how could I, when I

have done so myself? I am not implying that my Presbyterian church was *better* than my Anglican church, or that the Society of Friends is *better* than either: it was simply that as I changed, with age and other circumstances, the emphases of one became more meaningful to me than those of another. I am happy enough where I am for the present, but who knows where I shall end? With the Greek Orthodox, perhaps, wreathed in incense and taking the sacraments mixed together from a spoon? If we ever get one, vast, uniform church — will such a pilgrim's progress be possible?

The Church I have been talking about is the Church of tradition, of teaching and worshipping, and those are important functions. God pours down his grace – that is, his love – upon us, and unless we understand it and respond to it, that love is frustrated and in vain. That is why God needs the Church. He actually needs our response to his love, or the love which is God is incomplete – God is incomplete without the Church.

But I said the Church is also something else: it is community. That is obvious enough from its origins. St Paul spent his time visiting or writing to Christian communities all over the ancient world. It is quite clear that they did not exist solely to worship together and study the scriptures, but to care for one another, and that is something we rather lose sight of today. The social caring has been largely nationalised. Looking after the sick and the elderly, educating the young, relieving poverty and suffering – all were once in the hands of the Church but are now mostly (if inadequately) handled by the state. In a way, it is a triumph for the

Church to have converted the state to a philosophy of Christian caring, but in many parts of the kingdom the Church itself has been left feeling socially pointless. I fancy this is less true in Scotland, and I think that shows it need not be true elsewhere. There are still many gaps in the network of the Welfare State: I have mentioned moral education, and I would like to add here the care of the socially or mentally inadequate, people who simply cannot cope with modern life and who too often end up shuttling in and out of prison, where they do not really belong. It is the Church which should be providing a real community for them, not just an institution.

But if caring has been nationalised, faith has become privatised. People announce: "What I believe is my own business". And so it is, in a very serious way. Even the Catholic Church insists upon the primacy of conscience. But it insists, too, that it must be an *informed* conscience. I am afraid that "What I believe is my own business" often conceals a spiritual laziness and sometimes nakedness. Jesus and his followers argued all the time about their faith: they were never ashamed to expose it to others, and defend it. Another form of the remark is: "I find God walking through the heather – not crouching in the kirk"; and of course that is possible, too, though I wonder how often it really happens. Apart from anything else, very few of us are lucky enough to live within walking distance of the heather; and it is an inconvenient fact about the spiritual life that – like the athletic life or the life of music – it does require discipline, practice and regularity. That is really the reason for going to church. We can all *say* we will study the Bible at home and pray every morning for half an hour – but do we? Without regular practice, it is possible for the awareness of God to rust up, atrophy, become muffled in cobwebs. If anyone can think of a better way to keep faith in working order than by concentrating upon a church service, then the Church itself would like to hear from you.

But, as I say, the Church was not founded primarily as an instrument of worship. It was founded as a network of communities: "See that ye love one another – that ye care for one another", and unless church members really do that, they are setting aside the Lord's commandment and depriving themselves of half the meaning of the Christian faith. (If I really were a sacramentalist – which I am, in that I see *everything* as a sign of grace – then I would insist not only upon the sharing of bread and wine, but also upon the washing of feet, which is surely just as mandatory in scripture!)

The Christian community is also commanded to be open one to another, to speak plainly and without guile, and to accept others without cynicism. Yet most of us are terribly afraid of each other, afraid of other people's ideas, and afraid to reveal our own. We do not want to hear ideas with which we do not agree, though we pretend it is not because *we* might be deceived by them (you and I are much too wise for that), but because others less wise may be taken in. The Church is one community in which this should not be. It ought to be a community in which our hopes and doubts are not privatised, a community of openness and readiness to listen, a community of mercy and forgiveness.

It is also, frankly, a community of sinners and not a community of the virtuous. I get into fearful trouble by taking this too far and saying that I detest churches where everyone is righteous and sober and saved and certain, for that does not seem to me a church of real people at all. I like a church that is in the world and of the world, a church of doubters and drinkers and neurotics, who know what they are and confess it: confess that they are just like everyone else, except that they have been bitten by this God Thing which will not leave them alone.

I believe – and here comes more trouble – that Jesus actually preferred the company of sinners, partly because they were so much more fun at those parties he enjoyed giving; and because they were frank and open about themselves. The people he could not stand were the self-righteous – those who just knew they were saved. They had no place in his kingdom, because they thought they had no need of it.

Besides being lazy and selfish, privatised religion can also be shallow and banal. You find people basking in the private discovery that God is Love (or Electricity, or Evolution), or that Jesus Saves, and going no further. Which leaves them extremely vulnerable not only to more ingenious argument, but to the setbacks and failures which inevitably lie ahead for all of us.

How to come to terms with the suffering and failure that afflict men even under the reign of a loving God is a problem which has taken – and still takes – all the wisdom and prayer of generations of saints. And it is very hard to cope with privately. Even if you think you have found your own answers, you still need the traditions, teachings and authority of the Church to test them against. Every experimental scientist knows he must prove his discoveries to the orthodox establishment, or his time and efforts are wasted. It may even turn out that he has been deluding himself, and here is the ultimate danger of religion wholly divorced from the Church: it may go mad or bad, even positively evil. Nor is it enough to belong to a small, tightly-knit group which has convinced itself that it alone has the secret of salvation. The story of Christianity is full of demented prophets and bewitched followers, alienating themselves from the family of God as a whole by using a self-confirming code language. I repeat: the Church it not a secret society. It is an open society and the language it uses has been spoken openly and frankly for centuries.

The Church has never claimed to know every-thing about God. The Christian faith would have died long ago if it had had nothing more to say after the last "Amen" of the Book of Revelation. But when people come along with new revelations, the Church has some very clear tests to apply before it will accept them. Call this authoritarian if you will – though, goodness knows, it is extremely hard to get excommunicated today, and I have not seen a good heretic-burning for years – but I do think we need the Church to keep some kind of intellectual order among us. I am not too con-cerned about undermining the simple faith of the

common people, because I do not think a really
simple faith will admit the subtleties that would
undermine it. I am more concerned that new ideas
be given time to digest, so that what is good in them
may be absorbed and what is mere fashion have
time to wither and be rejected. In the end, truth
will prevail because it works and makes sense.
Even the most ancient heresies keep coming back
because they are *half*-truths: the heresy lies in
pretending they are the whole truth. Such worth as
they have will be lost if orthodox teaching either
suppresses them entirely or stands back and allows
them to pass without challenge. The important
thing is the challenge itself, which is good for both
sides.

I must confess that I have been directing my
remarks mainly to those among you who belong to
what I have called the Great Anonymous Church
of the Unchurched: people who sense a religious
dimension to their lives, who cannot do without
some kind of God-talk to express what they intuit
about life (a power or a pattern behind it), but who
seriously doubt whether the traditional churches
have anything to do with it. Who doubt, indeed,
whether it is even possible to talk to the churches
without surrendering one's integrity. I know, from
the people who come up and talk to me or who
write letters to me, that there is a secret
congregation – a Church behind the Church –
which probably outnumbers those who are on the
official rolls. Some of them are on the rolls, but
half-heartedly. They could not recite the creeds
without mental reservations. And it is such people
whom I especially value: people who are deter-

mined to be Christians, whether or not they pass
the Church's tests. To them I want to say that it *is*
possible, indeed it is necessary, to belong to the
Church without feeling guilty. Do not be put off by
its compromised history. Yes, it has committed all
too many of the crimes of which it stands accused.
But it is not, and cannot be, any better than the
human beings of which it is composed. The
Christian faith is not a magic spell for turning
sinners into angels, it is a lifebelt which can save the
sinner (if he clings to it) from drowning in his own
sins; saves him not by his merit, but by its
buoyancy, whoever he is. And just as we would
wish to be judged in the light of our circumstances,
so must we judge the Church. Since the days of
Constantine, it has been used and exploited by the
secular world, and it has compromised for the sake
of its own survival. Often it has compromised too
much: it has mistaken might for right; but I venture
to say that history would have been very much
worse without the Church's part in it. Without the
Church, we should today have no alternative to the
supreme value of the state. Much of the world –
where there is no Church – has no alternative, and
the result is plain to see. The moral tension under
which this country still lives – a necessary tension
that keeps us making choices, a tension between
individual liberty and social justice – is one derived
from the gospel and kept alive by the Church. The
Church itself swings like a pendulum, stressing now
the responsibility of the individual, now the welfare
of the community. But without the religious
atmosphere in which to swing, the pendulum would
have settled long ago on the side of secular

power – on the side of the National Interest as those who had power chose to define it.

If you ask the Man in the Street what he thinks of the Church today, you will get a strangely ambiguous answer. On the one hand you will be told that it is a lot of fairy tales for old ladies (as if old ladies were not the wisest among us). On the other, you will find a sentimental reluctance to see the Church die off. People still value the rites of passage – baptism, marriage, funerals – and there is still an instinctive folk-religion that draws people to pray in time of trouble, or to recognise Christ as more than just a very good man. In most of the English villages I know, it is easier to close down an underused telephone kiosk than an empty church. The Church still represents something the community knows it has neglected, but dare not lose. It is aware that its arches and graveyard and its somewhat antiquated liturgy stand for an intense investment of the past which we today cannot write off without cutting our own roots.

Do we need the Church, then, for purely sentimental reasons, or because the building provides an architectural focus for the neighbourhood? Those reasons stand, I think, along with the others I have mentioned. But the greatest single reason why the Man in the Street needs the Church is that he needs an alternative source of comment and criticism upon the secular world. He needs the prophecy – the speaking forth – that the Church has always given: a dangerous activity, perhaps, for it can always lapse into second-rate politics, but it has to be done unless the Church is to become just an unconvincing salesman for the world to come. I am not saying there *is* no world to come, but the fact that we know so little about it suggests to me that we are not intended to bother about it very much.

The Man in the Street needs the Church to help him cope with failure, to show him (through the world's greatest failure, upon the Cross) that the response to failure must be resurrection: the most positive out of the most negative, which is the precise opposite of the world's wisdom.

The Man in the Street needs the Church to show him that there *is* a moral order, that there is above all a choice: that we are not just life's victims, but its protagonists – its actors and doers. And the special thing about the Christian faith is that it does not merely command us to make choices in accordance with God's will, but offers us the strength to do so.

The Man in the Street needs the Church to show him that there is a God. How can it do this? The very free will with which God has endowed us means that there cannot be an irresistible proof compelling all men to believe in him. If there were, we could only fear God, not love him. No, the duty of the Church is to show men how they can gain their own experience of God (an experience which is far more common than many people suppose), and to confirm that experience by displaying the traditional stories about God, and by living, itself, as if there were a God. If it does that, God himself will glorify the Church so that his truth becomes manifest.

But I must conclude by repeating myself: the Church is not a hierarchy of ministers and priests. It is and always was the whole society of friends that call themselves Christians. Church-going as such has its value in exercising our spiritual faculties. But if we as the Church are to show forth God's will, we must show it not just in the kirk, but in the street. We must look for that of God in everyone we encounter, and address it with reverence. We must listen for the voice of the Spirit in every word we hear. We must search out sacramental grace in everything we see, and respond to it. Above all, we must choose – we must choose to choose – and not be washed along by the current of the day.

This does not mean that we must all plunge ourselves into mighty arguments about nuclear weapons and the Third World – though I shall be contemplating those in my next lecture. I think that we members of the Church often exhaust ourselves to despair by hammering too much at such issues and neglecting the incidents under our nose – encounters with our neighbours or family – which are far more important in developing our souls. Far more important, too, than listening to me any longer!

2

THE CHURCH IN THE WORLD

I concluded my first lecture in this series by hinting that Christians often exhaust too much of their energy in worrying about great issues which they are powerless to affect. I imagine that if the energy expended by British Christians in protest marches on behalf of South Africa, Chile and Poland could have been converted into kilowatt hours, it would have provided enough electricity to preserve several thousand old folk from hypothermia. All sorts of lessons could be drawn from that: notably that energy is not, in fact, transferable by a stroke of the pen; but what I have to do this evening is to restore the balance by admitting that the Church, as an institution, would be worth little if it could not look beyond its own doorstep. For it is charged, as Adam was charged, with the stewardship of the whole of creation, with loving its neighbour, not just itself.

The Christian faith is indeed about the salvation of the individual soul: but to what purpose, and in what context? Adam was alone in Eden for a very short time. Before long he had to start living and thinking in relation to others, and psychologists will tell you that everything we know about ourselves has to be bounced off our relationships with other people. So it is with churches and with nations. We are what we are in comparison and interaction with others.

But what place has the Church in this pattern? Can we not define ourselves in social, geographical, political and economic terms? Does the Church do anything but complicate and irritate the situation?

We are really back with the old argument about the Church and the Emperor Constantine. Did the gospel take over the Empire, or did the Empire subvert the gospel?

Personally I cannot see Constantine as a devoutly Christian figure. I think he was essentially a political opportunist. But in effect it was six of one and half a dozen of the other, and has continued so until quite recently. Church and state have compromised with each other, the Church needing the protection and authority of the state and the state needing the intellectual skills and sense of direction provided by the Church. On the whole, the Church has had the better end of the bargain, because its objectives have been far steadier than the state's. When you come to think of it, the state has mostly been run by unstable amateurs ("Here today and gone tomorrow" was the phrase immortalised by my colleague Sir Robin Day) while the Church's interests have been pursued relentlessly by a succession of trained and dedicated traditionalists. Compared with the churches, our political institutions are relative newcomers; and the churches have learned to adapt themselves to every twist and turn of the political dance – or rather, they have up till now. One might not wish to go quite as far as the

Orthodox Church in Russia, which has been prepared to make almost any concession in order to keep the Eucharist going behind the iconostasis, but given the choice between a wholly secularised society, a wholly theocratic one, and one that was half-and-half, I fancy most of us would be grateful for the latter. We must have the Church in the world, but I tremble at the thought of a world wholly the Church's. Wholly God's – yes; but I think we must leave room for God to define his own will and not presume to organise it all for him.

What I have just said may have shocked some of you, but I think it is worth standing by. Some people assume – without much hope that it will ever come true – that we should be working towards a world that is actually led by the Christian Church. In my last lecture I confessed to no great enthusiasm for a uniform Church in any case, and I must go further now and suggest that it would diminish God's access to mankind if his only way to our spirits lay through the Christian faith. Do we really suppose that Islam, Hinduism and Buddhism in particular would have survived to this day if they were of no use to the Holy Spirit?

Am I saying that Islam, Hinduism and Buddhism are "as good as" Christianity? I am not, partly because "as good as" is a meaningless phrase in this context, and partly because for me it is certainly not true, in the sense that not having been brought up in any of those other faiths I have no grounds for saying it is true. I simply do not know; though to me it seems unlikely. In practical terms, the Christian faith offers much greater flexibility, more chances of development and adaptation to local circum-

stances than the rest. But I think it is a necessary
characteristic of any religion to believe it is superior
to any other. I have no objection to people
changing their religion, if they are genuinely
convinced – though it may be sad when, by doing
so, they cut themselves off from the society they
were born into. A religion should deepen one's
sense of unity with one's fellows, not isolate one. If
we are honest, we will admit that we are Christians
or Muslims mainly because we were born in
Scotland or Pakistan.

And in Scotland, with its fine record of mission-
ary work (in Pakistan, among other places) I realise
that I must defend myself against the charge of
belittling that work. Did not Christ charge his
disciples to go forth preaching and baptising in his
name? Indeed he did, and he also charged them to
heal the sick, clothe the naked, visit the impris-
oned; and he warned them that some seed would
bear increase, some fall upon stony ground. It
seems to me entirely right that mission work today
should concentrate upon service, rather than
services, that we should look to the indigenous
ministry to cultivate the spiritual crop, and that we
should look still more to our own behaviour as a
Christian nation, if we are one, to preach by
example. Hypocrisy is a word I detest – it poisons
too many discussions, and I sometimes think the
only real hypocrisy is to accuse other people of
hypocrisy (for we all suffer from mixed motives):
but it ill becomes us to tinker with other people's
cultures when our own is in such a parlous state.

The Church in the world must be a humble
Church and a serving Church rather than a

lecturing Church. I am inclined to think it must also be a patient and waiting Church: waiting is a vocation we tend to overlook in our busyness. The Church should be open and available in its life of worship and prayer, and it should always keep one ear open for any call to serve. But it should beware of becoming a hectoring, bossy, interfering Church.

Is it not, then, to be a prophetic Church – speaking forth to society where it sees the will of God being flouted? Is it in no sense to be a political Church? The Biblical prophet was invariably a political figure as well as a religious one: no-one expected otherwise. Why should it be different today?

Here in Scotland, I am aware there is less controversy than there is in England over the right of the Church to give a lead in public affairs. I believe the English controversy is of fairly recent origin, in fact; and that when people say, "Keep the Church out of politics" they usually mean, "Confine the Church to Tory politics". As you may have heard, the Church of England is now accused of being the Social Democratic Party at prayer. But for centuries it was always part of the ruling-class establishment, and now that that establishment is divided along party lines (more drastically than it ever was before) the Church is bound to make some utterances that give political offence. That it is usually the Right which is offended only shows how deep the Right's assumption of Church support had become. The Marxist Left does not expect much of the Church anyway, so does not feel betrayed.

Let me state my own position on the Church in politics, and before that, on politics in general. You might label it Disillusionism or, as I would prefer, Realism; but what it comes down to is a charitable conviction that nobody can ever understand how the system works, and it is arrogance to pretend we can plan it. It is not that nothing can be done, but that much less can be done than it is opportune to admit, that it takes much longer to do anything, and that the situation will have changed anyway by the time measures to control what it used to be can become effective. One of the few heresies I recognise is the heresy that if only we can get the rules and structures right, our troubles will fly away. We all know they will not, because we all know the trouble is not really with the structures but with people. Which is why, very sensibly, we ignore the politicians' pleas to stop focusing on their personalities and concentrate on "the issues". Issues and structures are not unimportant, but they are incapable of making choices or knowing the difference between right and wrong. In the end, they are dependent upon people: sinful, fallible, fallen people.

This being so, it is important – within the bounds of what is practical – to keep choices open so that we can repent of our political sins and turn again towards what we hope is righteousness. The two beacons of righteousness which have long guided this kingdom have been Individual Liberty on the one hand and Social Justice on the other. Interestingly – though I would not wish to press the analogy too far – Individual Liberty has something in common with the spirit of the New

Testament, and Social Justice with the Old. But it is
hard to reconcile the two, and so the pendulum
swings to and fro and we pursue a somewhat zig-zag
course between them. Our system is, thank
goodness, no system: our socialists compromise
with capitalism, and our capitalists have a social
conscience.

Looking about us today, we can hardly claim that
this "no system" is triumphantly successful or
could not possibly be improved on. It is unjust to
the poor and the jobless and I happen to think it is
grossly negligent towards education. However, it is
relatively tolerant and humane, remarkably stable
and, compared with most of the world's nations,
abhors violence. If we will political change, we can
make it without people getting hurt, and there are
not many countries – even in Europe – where that
is true. To quote Yeats' bitter poem: "The beggars
may change places, but the lash goes on". In any
revolution, the poor suffer more than the
powerful – even those who are ejected from
power.

Now I yield to nobody in my mockery of
politicians. But if we should beware of their sins,
we should also be aware of their virtues. What I
said about the necessary confidence of religions in
their own rightness is probably true of political
parties also, and I have never met a politician who
would confess to any strain between his political
duty and his conscience. Most politicians really
believe they are right, and it is probably just as well
that they do not share my "Disillusionism" or we
would have no government at all. I do not agree
with Acton's dictum that "power tends to corrupt".

Whatever its faults, ours is not a corrupt political system, for it is not staffed by corrupt men and women.

One of the difficulties the Church has in the world today is that, deep in its heart, it is suspicious of Power. It is tempting to attribute this to memories of what the civil powers did to the Church – and to its Founder – in pre-Constantinian days; but I do not think that is the explanation. The Church should have much longer and happier memories of power shared with the state, a partnership still celebrated in the Anglican Book of Common Prayer. Only a few months ago, while attending a service in St George's Chapel, Windsor Castle, I was leafing through a nineteenth-century edition of the Prayer Book and was astonished to find it full of thanksgiving for deliverance from the Gunpowder Plot, for the suppression of "the late disorders" and sundry other expressions of solidarity with the Crown. Yet today the Church is virtually accused of treason for its lack of enthusiasm over the Falklands victory, and for sponsoring a unilateralist report on nuclear disarmament.

In neither case was it a simple matter of party prejudice: there was a fundamental suspicion of those in command of power, and it was less an example of the Church playing politics than a refusal by the Church to be played with by politicians, an insistence on rising above the political level.

There may be a trace of envy here. The Church has lost so much of its grip upon the world. As I was saying last night, education, administration, medi-

cine, science, the care of the infirm were once all in
the hands of the Church and have now become very
largely the work of the state. In some ways this is a
success for the Church: it has converted the state
into a caring institution. But as the state has taken
over these functions, the Church has lost power
and lost the very instruments through which it
could practise what it preached. Once again, this is
probably less true in Scotland than it is in England
and Wales, but throughout the kingdom I hear
young people asking: "What does the Church *do*?
It just talks – and in a language we can't understand."

As I said earlier, there is still plenty the Church
could do, many gaps in our social, educational and
cultural life that it could fill if it had the manpower
and the money. It would surely be to the advantage
of the state to adopt a more generous attitude
towards tax exemption for donations to charity and
the lifting of Value Added Tax on supplies used by
charities. But without much opportunity for action,
the Church is often tempted to talk even more in
the hope of influencing the powerful, and the result
often has an air of unreality.

Let me say at once that I am not, in principle,
opposed to the churches setting up working parties,
studying the issues of the day and publishing
reports. It is as well that somebody without a party
axe to grind should offer alternative views to those
of the government or opposition. But the churches
need to be sure that they have the brain-power to
command respect. Time was when they commanded the best brains in the country, but I am afraid
that is not necessarily so today. I have read reports

from church departments based on little more than
newspaper cuttings, reports which would not have
secured a poor degree at a minor university and
which (to the scandal of those who wrote them)
were rightly ignored by the national press.

The press has been equally right in giving
considerable publicity to the growing anti-nuclear
feeling among the British churches. The recent
report of the Church of England working party on
The Church and the Bomb is a case in point. It
was, in fact, produced by an ecumenical group of
great intellectual distinction and it falls far below
the group's own standards to dismiss the report as
the whining of a bunch of cowards.

I have come to this question because it is
probably the outstanding example of the Church
feeling compelled to strike an attitude in the world,
and because it raises the whole question of the
Church and Power. The Church, we have seen, is
largely powerless today. Does it appreciate suffi-
ciently that politicians are men with a vocation to
power, a difficult and demanding one?

I speak as one who, being a Quaker, has a
personal commitment to pacifism which makes me
naturally sympathetic to the working party report.
This, too, is difficult and demanding. It would have
been much easier, during the Falklands Expedi-
tion, to have followed the patriotic line and
justified the war. The war against Hitler has made
it extremely difficult to argue that evil should never
be physically resisted. I can only say that for me
pacifism is a personal vocation, like celibacy, which
I would not dream of urging upon anyone who did
not feel similarly called. One must take the

consequences oneself, one must not force them upon others, and one must attribute to those who fight the same sincerity. One can only hope that they know what they do.

Doubts about that lie at the root of the growing anti-bomb movement in the Church (and it is a movement quite as strong among Catholics as among Protestants). Giant strides have been made since those first horrific experiments over Japan, and the fact is nobody really knows what nuclear war would be like. The implication of the Bomb as deterrent is that it would be so dreadful for both sides that nobody will unleash it. But can we rely on that? It seems that we cannot even rely on the Bomb to deter fringe wars – they continue as merrily as ever in South East Asia, Afghanistan, the Middle East, the South Atlantic. You might have thought that, if the bomb really were a deterrent, a few dozen weapons on either side would suffice. But each side has thousands, and the cost is beyond all morality. We are talking about war on a totally different scale from anything in history, compared with which the indiscriminate bombing of World War Two was selective. We are talking about weapons which dominate those who claim to control them. Neither of the Great Wars in this century has developed as anyone expected. Their consequences were beyond any prediction. A third one . . . why should we believe that would be controllable?

You can see that I find it hard to understand how any Christian can contemplate justifying nuclear war or even the accumulation of nuclear weapons. The Church is steadily inching towards this position. And yet I have to ask if it is right to do so – if it is right to make those with the power to defend our freedom appear to be callous, insane, no better (in fact) than the power in the Kremlin? It is all very well to say that the Russians are not really aggressive, that they are only afraid of us; but anyone who thinks their idea of freedom remotely resembles *our* idea of freedom needs a trip to East Berlin. Pacifists may and do argue that nuclear destruction would be out of all proportion to the freedom it might preserve; but can they be sure? May they not underestimate the sacrifice that people are prepared to make, and have shown themselves ready to make before now? And despite the threats that have been made on both sides, we cannot be *certain* that a nuclear war *would* be unlimited and totally devastating. Dare we be paralysed by the fear that it would?

To a large extent there, I have been playing the Devil's – or rather the Bomb's – advocate. If the Church is to take a pacifist stand, it will find me here waiting for it. But I should be sorry if it moved too fast and arrived with no followers but a handful of clergy. If it must prophesy against the Bomb – and I think it must – it still has to stay with the people, and if possible with their rulers, and it must not cut itself off from them by climbing into a world of pure ethics.

There is, of course, a dilemma here, and it is one that discomforts the Church in the world all the time. For is it not charged with upholding ethical purity, before all things? But if it does, how can it come home with the man in the street who drinks a bit too much, fiddles his expenses and is occasionally unfaithful to his wife?

But the Christian faith is not primarily about being virtuous: it is one of its greatest handicaps that it has been saddled with that reputation. It is actually about being human, and that inevitably involves being a sinner. The speciality of the Christian faith is helping us to cope with sin, through the mechanism of Redemption, Repentance and Grace. Grappling with this the Church – which is itself sinful – cannot help getting its hands dirty. It must regard physical violence as a blasphemy against creation, but it must still send out chaplains to the armed forces. It may be appalled by government policy on divorce and abortion, but it must still minister to the Minister, as it must to prostitutes and prisoners and men who sell pornography. Like Pope John-Paul II, it must go to Argentina as well as to Scotland, and it must be able to talk to the Secretary of State for Defence as well as the Chairman of the CND.

The Church should permeate and infiltrate the world, not make a private collection of those it favours. What matters is not whether socialism is more Christian than capitalism, but that both should be influenced by Christianity, and that there should be Christians on both sides. In rather the same way, I am less interested in something called "Christian broadcasting" than I am in finding Christians broadcasting – and preferably they should not all be in one department labelled Religious Programmes, but in everything from News to Popular Music. For in the end, the best way of showing forth the Church in the world is to show that the Church is not its buildings and not its clergy, not even its services on Sunday, but its people out and about in their everyday lives, *being* Christians – which is being truly human according to God's will.

Is there no place, then, for the Word – the spoken message of the Church? Certainly there is a place, and as we all saw and heard when John-Paul was with us here – or Billy Graham for that matter – extraordinary numbers of people are hungry for it. In part I think this is due to sheer disillusion with the political word, the economic word, which has promised so much and delivered so little. Some of the Pope's words were hard words or at times, to some of us, theologically unacceptable: but there they were loud and clear and listened to, if by no means always obeyed.

For the Church in the world of today is no longer in any position to threaten its people with hell-fire. That does not work any more, and I have to report that I have failed dismally to provoke any of the Catholic priests I know into consigning me there. People today will talk back to the Church, and the Church will learn much by listening to them. It will learn, for example, that many of the deepest doctrinal issues which have exercised it for centuries – the Trinity, for example, or Justification by Faith – are of very little active concern to the average (perhaps untutored) believer. If these things do matter – and we may have varying degrees of enthusiasm for them – then there is surely a desperate need for a popular theology which people can understand.

The Church may stand for something ultimately changeless. The gospel is still with us, more reliably than almost any classical text. But you have only to read the Athanasian Creed – with its references to heresies that no longer bother us, and its silences about things that bother us a great deal – to realise that what has changed, and changes constantly if slowly, is the emphasis of the Church and its styles of thinking and expressing itself. We know that in the past the Church has emphasised prophecy of the future, the end of the world, the power of Satan, the promise of heaven, as if each were the dominant theme of scripture; and indeed I know people today who would underline one or another of those. And this, I believe, is the power of the scriptures – that there is something in them that speaks to the special condition of every generation. Things that have always been there, half sub-merged, rise to the surface as others sink back again. What the Church has to do now is to show the world what is there for this generation.

There are some who have looked into scripture, and into their conscience and experience, and found a so-called Theology of Liberation there: "He hath put down the mighty from their seat and exalted the humble and meek – the rich he hath sent empty away." Well, I can see the dangers of exalting a few passages in the gospel as if they were its whole message. But they – the Liberationists – are *there* among the poor of Latin America, and I am not. Can I in my comfort will that they should be as content with their discomfort? Must I snatch away from them such gospel as is alive for them, because they are sinners? Would their sin be more acceptable without it?

Again you may recall the uproar over the World

Council of Churches' grants for guerrillas in
Rhodesia (to which, incidentally, the British
Churches contributed almost nothing. It was not,
in any case, a fund to be used for weapons.) One
might bandy atrocities from side to side. But even
I, a pacifist, have to recognise that there are
Christians to Left and Right who do not share my
view that warfare cannot be justified. In fact, they
are the majority: they include most of my British
friends, people who dropped firebombs on Ham-
burg, people who ordered the shooting of anti-
British demonstrators in India. The Church cannot
wash its hands of people simply because they have
blood on theirs. War is the Church's shame and
failure, and it must never lose touch with those who
need to be brought to Peace.

How is it to make itself heard, though? I shall be
talking tomorrow about the Church in the Air, the
Broadcast Church. For the time being, I am more
concerned with how the Church is to make its
message *worth* hearing, for while people are
woefully ignorant abut the basic faith and its stories
they are unlikely to want to hear them unless they
see their relevance to their own lives. I said earlier
that Christianity was not primarily about making
people good: nonetheless, it seems to me that
without a religious foundation – a pattern of what
Man is intended to be – morality becomes mani-
pulable and contingent. The Church is in the world
to show that there are limits, and that compromise
cannot go on for ever.

I am not claiming that without the Church we
should have no standards of right and wrong at all.
There are certain standards – truth-telling, the

value of life, and sexual ordering in society – which are almost universal and recognised as belonging to Natural Morality. The classic values of *Stoicism* were taken over and added to by the Church. But all of these are to be justified, fundamentally, as making for the smooth running of society. Life is difficult enough at the best of times, but it becomes chaotic and unpredictable if people do not keep their promises, if life is treated as expendable, if sexual partners are unable to rely upon each other. Morality thus begins to appear as a set of rules designed for social efficiency, and even the Ten Commandments can be seen as essentially the rules of the Club of Israel, governing family and property rather than personal choice. And as we can see all too clearly today, in Western consumer society as well as the Marxist nations, the view of both these institutions can change drastically, dragging moral standards after it. If moral standards are set merely by what is expedient for the community, or to its pleasure, then it is only necessary for the ruling class, the party or the majority to redefine the aims of the community for what was wrong a generation ago to become right today.

And why not? Is that not progress? Inconveniently, sometimes it is. But there is a hard core which cannot be whittled down without undermining what I think is the foundation of the Christian view of mankind, and that is our free will: the demand that we *choose* to follow God's will for us, choose to respond to his love, and do not simply do what everyone else is doing because it is what is being done. How we discern that will is what the

D

Church endeavours to teach us. It knows much about the principles of the problem, because of its guardianship of scripture and its long case-history of the past. What it cannot always be sure of is the exact nature of the particular case, for what that comes down to in the end is a question of identity: Who are you really, who have you chosen to be? Only God knows whether you have chosen the pattern that he intended for you, whether you have the strength to resist the pressures pushing you away from it.

So I do not think the Church is in the world to denounce people for failing to be perfect. Let nobody pretend that the Church is perfect itself. What it is called upon to do is to point to its Founder as an example of the free will to choose: to choose to define oneself in terms disastrous by the world's standards, but in the end triumphant.

3

THE CHURCH IN THE AIR

In the first of these lectures I offered some reasons why the man and woman in the street as individuals needed the Church. In the second, I suggested its contributions to the wider world. In this final address I mean to retire to a narrower but more practical field and discuss the relationship between the Church and the medium of my choice: broadcasting. I have called this talk "The Church in the Air" rather than "of the Air" because I like the ambiguity: the image not only of the Church vibrating its message through the ether, but suspended above ground with no visible means of support.

If I have established some grounds for thinking that society and the individual do need the Church, we are indeed confronted with this gap between the Church and the world. For the world's need of the Church is not today acknowledged by the world; and if the Church is to overcome that resistance, it must argue with the world, it must show the world, it must tell the world, in short – it must communicate. And I am afraid that writing books – let alone giving public lectures – is going to communicate with only the small minority of those already converted. It will convey very little to that great majority who no longer read or attend lectures, but get or confirm their ideas from the screen and the loudspeaker.

So far as the United Kingdom is concerned, this is a crucial moment to consider the issue. The whole of broadcasting is about to be reshuffled and dealt anew. We in London have just seen the opening of a new television channel – Channel 4 – and to my mind the principal effect of this will be to break the mould of carefully balanced programmes, where every drop of acid is neutral-ised by a drop of alkali, and the result is a neutral, colourless fluid. I think we shall now get much more opinionated programmes in which a point of view is argued to the full, and the audience is credited with the ability to reject what it does not believe. In the distance we can also see the satellites going up, bringing us programmes from other countries beyond the control of British authorities. Under our feet, cable TV is about to start worming its way, with the potential to split up the audience into different tastes and tendencies – which may not be unwelcome to a government (a government of any party, I should add) which resents the independent power of giants like the BBC and ITN. Already with us is the phenomenon of the video-cassette, bringing us everything from education to pornography. Put together, all these developments are bound to have a revolutionary effect both on the economics of broadcasting – how it is to be paid for – and upon the sheer ability of people to choose. Up to now, our governments have been fairly successful in relating the two, in preserving financial viability by limiting choice: but they will be very hard put to it in future. One ally they have had in the past is the concern of those with power to preserve moral standards. Television is thought – I say "thought" because I am not wholly convinced it is so – to have a unique influence over those standards. Certainly the Church believes it has, which is why this junction of events is seen as crucial for religious broadcasting.

For sixty years, the Church has received privileged treatment from the broadcasting authorities. There is still an unofficial Sunday ghetto for programmes of worship, hymn-singing and moral uplift on television; while the BBC's "Daily Service" on Radio 4 is one of the longest-running and least changed of regular programmes anywhere in the world. It was started as the result of a one-woman campaign launched by a lady in Watford – resisted at first on the grounds that any form of worship that might be devised was bound to offend more listeners than it pleased and thus to create that phenomenon most dreaded of BBC officials, namely Trouble. Miraculously, though, a form was devised and has hardly been altered since. The Daily Service is ecumenically approved and is conducted by speakers ranging from a Roman Catholic laywoman to a radical Methodist minister. I have to say that it strikes me as the dreariest kind of deep-frozen Anglicanism – without guts, without joy, without any incentive to do anything but sit back and let it go by. I know there are many people (though, if truth be told, a declining number) who love it. Even hint at changing it, and there is an outcry. But it seems to me its very changelessness has become a symptom of its harmlessness: it is token Christianity that gives comfort to a few, but no real trouble to anybody. Perhaps "trouble" is not precisely the right word – though I think the Church, at a time like this, ought to be saying things that trouble the world. What worries me most is that this cool piety offers so little to *involve* its listeners. It has become almost a Tibetan prayer-wheel that mechanically does our praying for us, while we go away and do something else.

I am aware that those responsible for these services are concerned, too. They do not want to pull the prayer-mat away from under those who devoutly kneel upon it – in any case, there would be a fearful battle over any alternative – but they would like to help the Church to communicate with a wider, largely neglected, audience.

The religious broadcaster has to be extremely careful about how he practises his trade. There was a time when it was sufficient to be religious to be allowed to broadcast. But while it is possible to write badly about religion and get away with it under the shelter of the religious press or the religious bookshops, the religious broadcast has to stand direct comparison with the other programmes surrounding it. If it is boring, clumsy and incompetent, no matter how sound it is doctrinally people will not take it seriously. I hope it is true to say that most of the religious broadcasting done in the United Kingdom is now made as professionally as drama, sport or light entertainment – though it has to be confessed that not as much money is available, and programme planners tend to regard religion as a minority interest to be tucked away outside peak viewing times. And they are probably right: it *is* a minority interest, and here the religious broadcaster comes up against the second horn of his dilemma. He would like to make converts, in some sense, and if he is of an evangelical tendency he may even say that his job is to spread the gospel. But is that how his network sees it? I think not. It is not just that broadcasting executives have become secularised, and see no more reason for converting people to Christianity than they do for converting them to vegetarianism: they are well aware that the religious hard sell – whether High Church or Low – embarrasses and antagonises even the semi-religious.

One example of this is the "Thought for the Day" type item, of the kind you can hear in your morning magazine on Radio 4. Down in London, at any rate, this is a spot much prized by the religious broadcasters and it probably has the largest audience they get – thanks to the knock-on effect of the material surrounding it. But often it stands out like a sheep in a herd of goats: one minute we are listening to a roundup of the tabloid press, the next minute a bishop is talking about martyrdom, and the next John Timpson is turning (with some relief) to a story about the closing of the last cinema in Dover. In editorial terms, "Thought for the Day" does not fit. It jars, it jolts, it sounds like an Ave Maria at a rock concert, and the battle for its survival is continuous. Were it not for the heavy artillery of the churches, lined up in support across the road from Broadcasting House, it might have been dislodged long ago. Not (I hasten to add) that it is without influential protectors within

Broadcasting House itself. But keeping the Church's flag flying on that three-and-a-half minute spot is rather like maintaining a presence on the Falkland Islands.

The future of the big Sunday worship programmes may seem more assured – after all, they are only once a week, usually in time that nobody else seems to want. But just because worship is so important to the Christian, they are the programmes which worry the broadcaster most of all. He knows that putting a microphone in a church during a service – or even wheeling in two or three cameras – provides neither real broadcasting nor a real service. The viewer and listener is not, in fact, a member of that congregation; and if you are a sacramentalist, the deficiencies become painfully obvious. You can mess about with the liturgy, rehearse the congregation and drag in extra voices from ten miles around, but the thing is actually a fake. There are actually training courses for ministers who are going to conduct broadcast services, but it is a theatrical impossibility to address yourself both to the live congregation before you and to the invisible congregation of ones and twos watching and listening at home. It is the difference between addressing a public meeting and talking to a friend over the telephone. Furthermore – and here I speak, naturally, of those decadent churches south of the border, rather than of the One True Kirk! – the art of preaching is itself in sorry decline.

The search goes on for some kind of structured worship that is not religious voyeurism but valid in broadcasting's own terms. I find it very hard to see how this can be anything but private, or at best involve more than a small group, in the very nature of the medium. Some of the best religious broadcasting I have heard has been in the form of "meditation out loud": one person leading the thoughts of those other ones listening. On television, there have been two or three series of sitting-room Eucharists, with a family breaking bread together before the camera and inviting the viewer to do the same on his side of the screen – not a true Eucharist, I suppose, but at least an attempt to forge a sacrament in television's own terms, and strangely powerful to those who have played a part in it.

But can television construct its own visual language of worship, make its own icons? Or must it be dragged down by the fact that it is inevitably a medium once removed from the reality: that there is no "real presence" in any sense? I must say, as one who worships in the telepathic atmosphere of a Quaker meeting – a form of worship whose long silences make for very bad broadcasting – I am driven to confess that no broadcasting of worship can be a substitute for physical presence at worship. We may recall the real thing for those who cannot be there, but I for one would deplore it if we ever became accepted as the real thing.

In recent years, religious broadcasters have tried hard to come out from under the Gothic arches and inhabit more up-to-date premises. There has been a considerable, and often distinguished, output of documentary and current affairs programmes made by the religious departments and designed to appeal to the general public's instinct for the

meaning behind life. Many of them have been
programmes made by Christians from a Christian
point of view, rather than programmes directly
about Christianity; an approach which has been
criticised for trying to sugar the pill or smuggle in
piety in disguise. I must say, I would regret that as
much as I would the attempt to sugar or smuggle in
Marxism. But I think, too, we must beware of the
tendency to reject programmes *because* they have a
religious content. To cite my own work, for
convenience, I have made programmes about the
life and problems of the English church organist,
about death and the disposal of corpses, about
Latin American Liberation Theology, and about
the Orthodox churches of the East. All of them, I
hope, were well made, all of them interesting from
the human point of view, and all of them
inconceivable without the religious dimension.

And yet they all depended, to a large degree,
upon the readiness of the listener to accept a
certain amount of churchliness and God-language;
and what many church-people are demanding of
broadcasting today is that we in the business go
further and reach out to those who are not in the
Church. Church-people tend to believe that we in
the media have somehow robbed the churches of
their congregations and that it is up to us to bring
them back again.

I would deny this in two stages. For a start (and I
have written and spoken about this elsewhere) I do
not think the mass media are nearly as influential as
people suppose. I think they are just part of the
circulation of ideas, the means of communication
not the message; and I think what actually happens

in the world is far more important than what we in the media say about it. We did not invent the hydrogen bomb or the IRA, unemployment or inflation, the Falkland Islands or the weather. And when it comes to the formation of opinion, I think the most one ever achieves is to articulate, with professional skill, what people are already thinking but do not know how to express so well. Thus, if the media have downgraded the Church, it is because they sense that the public has already lost interest.

Which brings me to the second stage of my defence. Believe me, the mass media are constantly on the lookout for Good News: win the pools, discover a cure for cancer, marry the Prince of Wales and the front page is yours. All the media demand is evidence of something significant happening, and if they show little interest in the churches today it is because there is so little of that to show. The churches talk a good deal, and some of that talk is prayer, but they do not often do very much. You may retort that it is not their purpose to do things: that their purpose is to praise God and save souls, and that may be true. In which case perhaps the churches should look elsewhere than the media, for I imagine it is very rare for a soul to be saved by television.

That is what I imagine, but across the Atlantic there is a flourishing department of the communications business that thinks I am wrong. The so-called "Electronic Church" is booming, and bringing in something like two-hundred-and-fifty million pounds a year. At the bottom end, all you need to do is buy time on a local commercial radio station, read a bit of gospel, preach a bit of anti-communism, and make a fervent appeal for money to carry on the good work, and you're in business – literally. At the top end, you can build yourself a private university with its own television centre and put out coast-to-coast services of faith-healing. If anyone thinks this is typically American and could never happen here, let them remember that it is only a logical development of the kind of roving evangelism that used to be common in Britain. Could it happen here? Would it be possible, for example, for an evangelist to buy time on a cable TV channel? I gather that churches and political parties are likely to be excluded from doing so. The British Council of Churches seems anxious to preserve the present ecumenical approach to religious broadcasting. But again, in America, there are already Catholic, Episcopalian, Mormon and Jewish networks available, and if they choose to start bouncing their programmes across the world by satellite transmission, I do not see how they can be kept out. It remains to be seen, of course, whether anybody will watch them and whether they will do anything but harden the converted in their isolation and convince the uncommitted that religion is not for them.

The longer I work in the field of religious broadcasting, the more convinced I become that it is not and cannot be a substitute for the living local congregation. That is not to say that I am satisfied with congregations as they are – some are magnificent, some are dead from the knees up – but whatever they are, broadcasting can only be a supplement to what they do. It can give them a certain confidence, a certain courage and sense of importance, by circulating ideas among them and registering that they are as important to the national life as sport or politics. But much of what church-people expect religious broadcasters to do, like raising moral standards or winning souls for Christ, can only be done by individual Christians in their daily lives, by Christian parents above all, together with Christian ministers, Christian elders, Christian friends and teachers. They, not we, are the Church.

What then is there for an amateur theologian like myself to do? I propose to end this lecture with an apology and a reproach: an apology for my own activities, and a reproach to the institutional Church which has left this gap for me to fill.

Almost two years ago, a colleague of mine – a Christian radio producer – remarked to me, "You know, we go on putting out programmes about the Christian faith as if people knew what it was: and they don't any more. They don't learn it at their mothers' knees, they don't learn it at Sunday School or the Religious Instruction Class; and if we don't tell them, nobody will." And so a series of thirteen programmes called "Priestland's Progress' was born.

Its success was measurable: we quadrupled the audience for the time of day, we sold some two thousand complete sets of the series on tape and more than fifty thousand copies of the book. About twenty thousand people wrote in to us about the programmes. None of which would impress a popular disc jockey, I suppose, but for a course of pretty tough listening, late at night, on Christian theology, it was sensational.

I am very well aware of the defects of the series.
The theology was derivative and often vague – as
the Catholic newspaper, *The Universe*, remarked,
there was "Too much Priestland and not enough
progress". There were certainly not enough
women among the people we interviewed, nor
enough young people or laity. Perhaps there were
not enough conservative evangelicals either
(though some of these flatly refused to co-operate),
and none at all from the Moonies, Rosicrucians and
Snake Handlers. For there are limits, and since we
were trying to offer a so-called "Plain Man's Guide
to the Christian Faith" we had to keep near the
middle of the road, and avoid the more confusing
and aggressive side-tracks. Above all, we were
working on a very limited budget, far too little
time, and a staff of two-and-a-half men and a
girl – the half man being also the vicar of five
Hertfordshire parishes.

Radio, I believe, is a much more serious medium
for ideas than television (though not as good as
print). Personally, I find working for radio less
guilt-provoking than television, partly because it
costs so much less to make and partly because
almost every minute you devote to radio is
productive: you can either be writing a script,
recording it or editing it. Working for television is
largely a matter of waiting helplessly while a dozen
men and women aim things at you, and then
throwing yourself into a brief burst of action which
usually has to be repeated so often that you become
bored with it before the technicians are satisfied.
And it is all so expensive – and yet so ephemeral –
that my puritan soul keeps muttering that televi-

sion is inherently and irredeemably sinful, like caviar or attar of roses. Goodness knows, radio is no more durable – it rushes in at one ear and out at the other, leaving at best two or three ideas behind – but at least it is cheap and cost-effective.

The feed-back from "Priestland's Progress" indicated that I had two rather personal congregations among the public. One is what I call the Grey Fellowship of the Depressives: people who ought to be helped by faith but often are not, are frequently badly injured by it. Having been of the fellowship myself, until I was rescued by a stern Jewish psychiatrist, I know something of how oppressive the contemplation of the Cross can be.

Perhaps more important (and sometimes overlapping) is what I have already referred to as the Great Anonymous Church of the Unchurched. They are people for whom Jesus has a profound fascination, people with a real spiritual awareness and direct experience of the divine about which they do not like to talk, for fear of being thought neurotic or naïve. And as a result of their reluctance to talk, they fancy they are alone in the world, when in fact they are part of a widespread company, a company which finds little or nothing in the Church to reflect its experience and so keeps away from the Church.

These are people who increasingly lack the basic grounding in the faith which professional church-people still assume. Even if they could find the courage to talk about faith, many members of the Anonymous Church would not know how to express it, or do not believe that church-people

would understand them if they tried. They feel
alienated from the Church and suspect that even if
they approached it they would be refused admis-
sion because of their ignorance of the right
passwords.

One of the main purposes of "Priestland's
Progress" was to discuss some of those passwords
with leading church-people and find out if they
really were so forbidding. I remain dubious about
what lay people might call dogma, and along with
many outsiders am suspicious of any faith that
presents itself as a system of unreasonable certainties. The point I tried to make throughout my series
was that Christianity today is rather a system of
reasonable uncertainties. By "reasonable" I do not
necessarily mean "logical". I know very well that
faith involves heart and guts as well as head, and
that we are constantly confronted with mysteries,
but I do not think our faith is thereby unreasonable. I think it grows, it develops, it changes
even – and that we can all talk about it as freely as
we can discuss politics, economics, sex, death and
many other things which were once hardly men-
tionable in polite company.

I will not bore you – or risk reducing the sales of
my book – by rehearsing all the main themes of
"Priestland's Progress", but I will offer you a few
encapsulated slogans from it as examples of the
kind of thing it was possible to say without being
struck by lightning from above; of the kind of thing
which evidently spoke to the needs and instincts of
the Anonymous Church. The professionals among
you will doubtless have misgivings about some of
them, but I would beg them to bear in mind that old

theological dictum: "Doctrine is only an alternative to silence".

"If Jesus was not God – he is now" – that is how I cut the Gordian knot of the divinity of Christ, and I suppose some of you will see it as another form of the so-called "myth" of God incarnate. Be that as it may, it helps me out of the morass of argument about who Jesus may have thought he was and lands me squarely in the fact of who I know he is now.

I was deeply affected, too, by another line of thought which I suppose is fashionable, that of the weakness and suffering of God. I have come to see the Cross as – above all – a sign, a showing forth of God's solidarity with Man in suffering and weakness: "I am like you – I am like this – indeed, I am so like this that so far as you can ever know, I am this."

I have been obsessed also with the love of God in the supreme gift of free will, and with the consequence of that loving gift being the inevitability of sin. I am obsessed with the indestructibility of God's loving forgiveness: to me, the love of God means that, fundamentally, the universe is on our side, if only we will contemplate it and go with it, not against it. I am obsessed with the notion of doctrine as a tool that we use, not as an idol we worship. And I am obsessed with the idea of sacraments as a two-way language: God saying something to us, and we responding back to him.

The earliest response we received to all this contained a good deal of gospel-thumping: my favourite was a postcard depicting two rattlesnakes hissing at each other, with the caption: "BBC

E

wants a bigger licence fee to finance Priestland's
blasphemy." A letter from Clapham Common
declared: "I wish you wouldn't talk about Religion,
but get back to the Bible and to Jesus. Tell people
that Jesus died on the Cross for your sin and for
mine – that is all that matters." A listener in
Devon complained: "Today's programme left me
absolutely shattered. I feel my room needs disin-
fecting. To serve the Lord Jesus Christ as you have
done is an outrage. I am a member of the Church of
England and a committed Christian!"

From Liverpool came the admonition: "Your
series 'Priestland's Progress' may have caused
much confusion among many listeners, except
those committed Christians like myself who are
indignant over the sceptical and flippant treatment
of basic Christian truths. While some of the people
you have interviewed have defended those truths
well, many others have a non-committal approach
verging on the heretical." Another Northerner
wrote: "The most irritating aspect of the series has
been the pompous pseudo-intellectual comments
made in the interviews. These have demonstrated a
degree of unbelief astonishing and indeed alarming
in one with such an influential position. It is
obvious that the challenges posed by Christianity
caused considerable embarrassment to you, and
but for the prayers of the faithful, Satan could be
having a field-day."

Well, I think Satan has a field-day whenever
people stop asking questions and switch off their
brains. But my flagellation continued, especially
when I said that I could not believe that entry to
heaven would be reserved exclusively to card-

carrying members of the Christian churches. A West Country listener wrote: "To say that believers of other creeds, e.g. Muslims, Marxists, Mormons, Buddhists, etc., can go to the Father without acknowledging Jesus is nonsense. It denies the gospel. They do not worship the same God. From Exeter I was listening to 'Priestland's Progress', and I was amazed at God's tolerance of people like you. I believe the Bible to be the inspired word of God."

So did a listener in Shropshire: "Your series will be useless unless you face up fearlessly to the full implications of the New Testament Commandment, 'Thou shalt love God and thy neighbour', then you will find that Christianity is basically very simple. You are doing it no service, quite the reverse, if you present it as so vague and complex that no-one can gain assurance from studying it. 'Thou shalt love', the basic simplicity of this central law is undeniable."

Well, yes, but perhaps too simple. For it leaves me wondering what exactly it means "to love one's neighbour", how one gets the strength to love, how one copes with failure of love, rejection of love, how one is forgiven. I might have told that West Country listener that I was doing my best to love my Buddhist and Mormon neighbours – but I do not think he would have forgiven me.

My critics made their points, and good luck to them. They already had their reward and they certainly did not need me. Very soon they reached the same conclusion themselves, for that kind of letter rapidly fell away as they (presumably) stopped listening in disgust. Then, as I did two episodes on Sin and the meaning of the Cross, I started getting wave after wave of letters from the Depressives.

One came from Worcester: "As a middle-aged fellow depressive, how I agree with you about the Church and our affliction. I am still a regular church-goer, but I often wonder why. My real breakthrough moments of truth have come not because of anything connected with the Church, but from true psychiatric treatment. I expect I shall stay where I am, though, while holding some views that would horrify some of my neighbours in the pew. As you know, one of the delights of the Church of England is that you can believe more or less anything and still stay with it." (That, by the way, was far from being the intention of Elizabeth I and the authors of the Thirty-nine Articles!)

From St Albans came this: "My guilt came at me from every side: home, school, church, old Bible-thumping aunts. I knew before I even went to school that there was no hope for me. I was a goat, and at the Last Judgment I would be told 'I knew you not'. But I still thought the system unfair. At the end of school one day – it was a convent – my sister and I found one of the nuns crying about us, because she said we were nice children but surely going to Hell because we were not Catholics. I had had enough of that God." And the writer goes on: "Despite all my help from the Almighty, I cannot go to church any more. I cannot go back to that battering ram, not even if they say the same thing in modern words. I have never been able to feel that God could or does love me. It would be nice if he could. I have never felt forgiven, nor could I understand how Jesus could say 'Forgive them, they know not what they do'. I don't understand Jesus at all."

Somebody responsible for that woman's spiritual upbringing should have a terrible burden on their conscience. Could it have been a member of the clergy? I quote from somebody attending a discussion group in Surrey: "At our second meeting, the only clergyman in our group asked, 'What value do these talks have for Christians? The only test is whether they increase our faith.' Yet he was speaking to Christians who clearly wanted to understand better the jargon they hear in Church, and who were in turns stimulated, surprised and helped by your programmes. How can church people shake off the grip of church structures, especially the clergy, limiting how we see and respond to Jesus to their own unquestioning terms. It is in flat contradiction to the openness of Jesus towards all who came to him. I think it is this lack of openness which repels so many from the Church."

A letter from Oxford: "Many of us find church services a complete put-off, and aggressive Christians an even greater put-off. Often one is left feeling this an exclusive club to which one will never be admitted. The God-botherers leave us in no doubt we are sinners of the worst kind. Their lack of charity and thought makes one rush for the safety of agnosticism."

An agonised writer from Edinburgh – after confessing that such God-botherers were often the most outstanding people he knew – demanded: "But how can I join them without committing mental suicide?" And I know what he meant.

But certainly the most entertaining letters I received came from the out-and-out atheists. "You have not stated," boomed one from Suffolk, "on what evidence you believe there *is* a God. When providing evidence, please don't quote the Bible or the Koran, with which I am fully familiar. All religions are based on hearsay, imagination, wishful thinking and the constant cry for God to give us something for nothing."

Then there was the distinguished psychiatrist from Middlesex: "If Christian faith involves belief in a God who intervenes, how is the idea of a loving God to be squared with the horrors of natural disaster? The churches must face such anomalies rather than hiding behind the reassuring statement that God is Love. What, in the context of the actual cosmos, does that phrase mean?" (Actually, I find it strange that so distinguished a man should think this a major stumbling block. Like so many atheists, I fancy he thinks we believe in a kind of God we do not, in fact, believe in: God the tinkerer, magician and nursemaid.)

Another atheist, from near Windsor, reckoned he had found my Achilles heel: "Now Gerald, here's the nub of it – it's MONEY, filthy lucre! I need it, you need it, the Cosa Nostra and the ecclesiastical hierarchy need it (and Boy! have they got it!). And entirely without offence, dear Gerald, you make a very good living out of the Christian mumbo-jumbo. Your nonsense about free will is pernicious: God simply gave me a way to damn myself. My heredity, my environment have made me what I am. And what does he do? He damns me! God has made me to burn. The eternal potter makes a pot – it's a rotten pot, it doesn't fit his eternal criteria. So what does he do? Does he chuck the clay back, recycle it and start again? No, he says it's damned, and he makes the poor goddamed clay suffer eternally. He could have made it perfect. It's a mystery, you say? It's not just a mystery, it's nonsense."

But there were stimulating letters from believers, too. A licensed lay-reader, a lady, living near Oxford wrote to me: "I am bruised all over from the clobberings of shiny-faced charismatics, Bible-spouting evangelicals and condescending Anglo-Catholics, all pityingly referring to the poor, disproven, outmoded and shallow liberal like me. The rehabilitation your series has given us is sweet, and I hope it lasts."

My mailbag was by no means all hostile, though I am too modest – or rather too suspicious of my own conceit – to read out much of the favourable heap. Perhaps the most dear to me came from the wife of a well-known television figure, who I might call Roger. "Roger and I," wrote his wife, "move in circles where to be known as believers, let alone Christians, is to be marked out as simple-minded or hypocritical. Quite simply, your series gave us the courage to stand up and be counted; for we know now that we are not alone."

Indeed they are not, but the reproach is, they are outside the churches; they are writing to me, when they should be turning to the clergy, for it is so much easier for them to write to a faceless personality whom they more or less trust but do not actually have to confront. I have to ask the clergy, Why are you so forbidding? Why are intelligent and spiritually worthwhile people so reluctant to consult you on your own speciality?

For me the implications were and are daunting. I had thought that I was engaged in a marginal form of support for the Church; and then I found that people were turning to me as a substitute for the Church itself. You may say that this was merely a product of the modern obsession with the media: if it is on radio or television it must be better than the product at our own front door. But I find that unconvincing. Real people, living institutions, must always be more effective than electronic shadows if they are alive and well. One pastoral priest or minister is worth a dozen media gurus like me. But it seems that the hungry sheep look up and are not fed, and so they turn to the shadows. People like me came into the pulpit, thinking that we were merely wiring it for sound, and found ourselves staying on to conduct the entire service.

What are we to do? I, for one, have backed away from the job, partly because I know I am not worthy, qualified or equipped for it. If I had brushed those objections aside and embraced the calling whole-heartedly, what would it have become? A ministry of worship – but, as I have described already, how are we to worship convincingly when we are split up into thousands of separate homes? A ministry of teaching – but what right has the professional broadcaster to stand forth and say, "This is the faith"? A ministry of counsel – but although it is heartbreakingly clear to me that there are many thousands out there who are crying for help, how can we be any better than a magazine agony aunt guessing at a few words of comfort?

I and some of my colleagues have dreamed of a Church of the Air, perhaps based in some redundant church building and stuffed with studios, electronic gadgets and secretarial staff, churning out worship and meditation and pastoral advice. Even supposing we could finance such a venture and persuade the institutional churches to countenance such a rival, the dangers of it would be horrific. Somebody like *me* might come to rival the Moderator, the Archbishop and the Cardinal put together – not because he had been elected, qualified or ordained, but simply because he had the gift of the gab. And it would not be a real church, a society of friends knowing and caring for each other, but a plastic network of people who happened to switch on at the same time.

I, as a religious broadcaster, say emphatically that I do not wish to take the place of the Church; and I warn the Church that it must save itself from people like me. If people turn to me for help and advice, I can do no other than give it, but I know that I am no better than a temporary stop-gap. As a church, I am a phoney. What the Church must do, I think, is to do what the broadcasters cannot do: to love and care for its members as individuals, to be a community for them and for their neglected neighbours. That is not to say it should reject broadcasting. It should take very seriously its local broadcasting outlets, and use them as support for its living work.

The ministry of the air is something that every preacher should learn to cultivate: but, then, the ministry itself is something the Church must reconsider. Does it want a ministry of the people – like a Greek village, which nominates one of its members for ordination by the bishop? Or does it want a ministry of the elite, of the excelling? – in which case it must ask itself why the truly excellent no longer come forward. These are alternative ways, and I am not prepared to say here which I think is the better (after all, I belong to a church which has no set-apart ministry at all). What I do say to you is, beware the Church in the Air: make fast the Church upon Earth.